F U N
with
PAPER

F U N
with
PAPER

PAULINE BUTLER

JENNA BOOKS

Published by East Coast Marketing
Jenna Books
1350 Blue Hills Avenue,
Bloomfield, CT 06002

© Salamander Books Ltd, 1994
129-137 York Way,
London N7 9LG,
United Kingdom.

ISBN 1-85600-019-2

CREDITS

Editor: Jilly Glassborow

Designer: Patrick Knowles

Photographers: Mark Gatehouse and Jonathan Pollock

Craft adviser: Leslie Thompson

Typeset by: SX Composing Ltd., Rayleigh, Essex

Color separation by: Scantrans Pte. Ltd., Singapore

Printed in Belgium by: Proost International Book Production

Contents

INTRODUCTION

Paper is cheap to buy and great fun to play with. Most of the designs in this book are made with brightly colored construction paper that you buy in art supply stores. This kind of paper is best because it's strong and folds well. You will also need tracing paper so that you can trace the patterns from the back of the book, plus paper glue and scissors. For safety, always leave your scissors closed after using them.

Tracing Patterns Using a soft, sharp pencil, trace the pattern shapes from the back of the book. Now turn your tracing face down onto your colored paper and redraw over the outlines, pressing down firmly. The shapes will appear on the paper.

Fans are easy to make from pleated paper

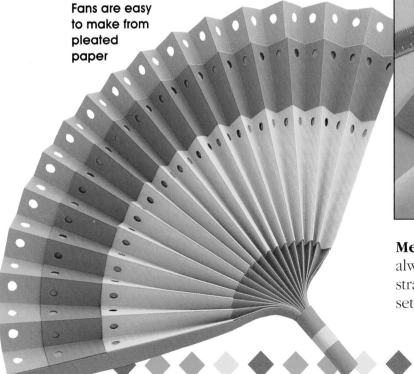

Measuring When drawing rectangles, always measure carefully and keep lines straight using a ruler. Draw corners with a set square to make sure they're square.

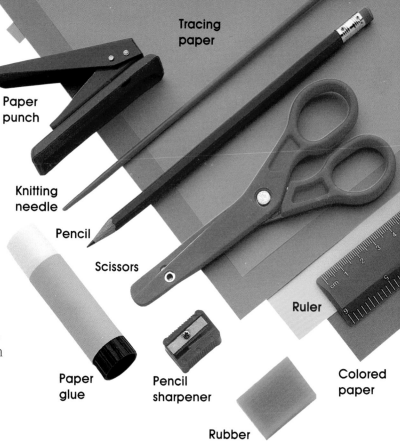

Tracing paper

Paper punch

Knitting needle

Pencil

Scissors

Ruler

Paper glue

Pencil sharpener

Rubber

Colored paper

Punching Holes When using a paper punch, remove the plastic backing and hold the punch upside down as shown so that you can clearly see your mark through the hole.

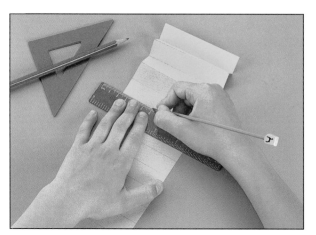

Folding To make a neat fold, first score your paper – make a crease in it – as follows. Lightly mark the fold line with a pencil and ruler. Then redraw along the line with a knitting needle, pressing down firmly. Fold the paper along the crease.

Curling Paper Strong paper, such as construction paper, curls quite easily. Simply stretch it gently across a slim pencil or knitting needle as shown to make it curl.

PAPER FLOWERS

Create these beautiful summer flowers from brightly colored paper. They make a perfect gift for a member of your family or a special friend. You will find the patterns for the leaves, petals, and stamens (flower centers) on page 28.

1 Trace all the pattern shapes with a pencil. Turn your tracing face down onto the colored paper and retrace over the outline. Trace two leaves for each flower. Now cut out all the shapes.

YOU WILL NEED

Pencil

Tracing paper

Scissors

Compass

All-purpose glue

Black poster paint

Paintbrush

Plant support stick

Cotton ball with center hole (you can buy these in art supply stores)

Construction paper in two bright colors, and bright green for the leaves

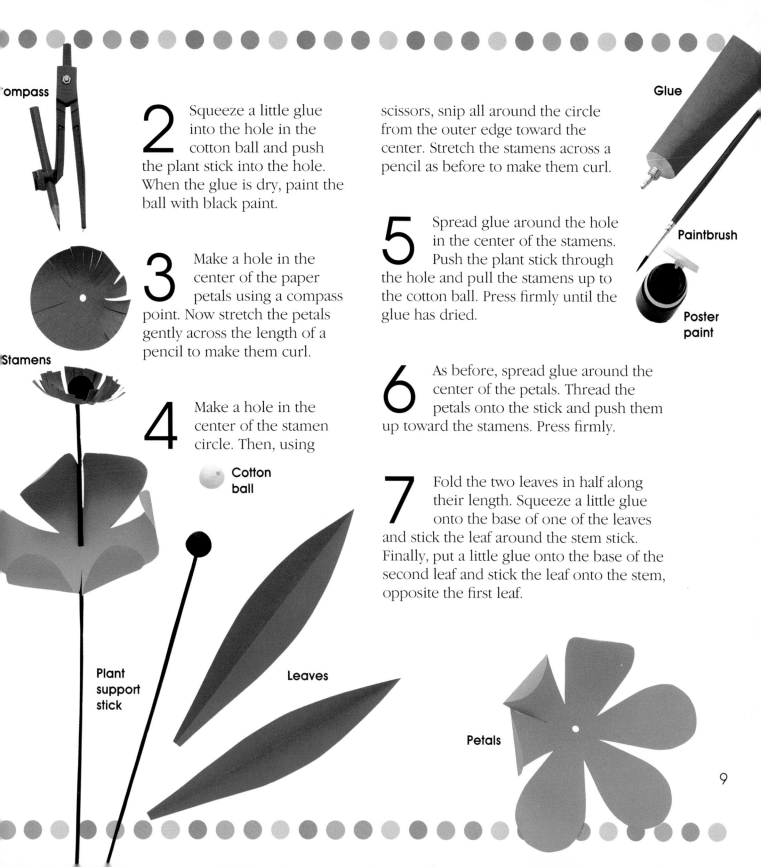

Compass

2 Squeeze a little glue into the hole in the cotton ball and push the plant stick into the hole. When the glue is dry, paint the ball with black paint.

3 Make a hole in the center of the paper petals using a compass point. Now stretch the petals gently across the length of a pencil to make them curl.

Stamens

4 Make a hole in the center of the stamen circle. Then, using

Cotton ball

Plant support stick

Leaves

scissors, snip all around the circle from the outer edge toward the center. Stretch the stamens across a pencil as before to make them curl.

5 Spread glue around the hole in the center of the stamens. Push the plant stick through the hole and pull the stamens up to the cotton ball. Press firmly until the glue has dried.

6 As before, spread glue around the center of the petals. Thread the petals onto the stick and push them up toward the stamens. Press firmly.

7 Fold the two leaves in half along their length. Squeeze a little glue onto the base of one of the leaves and stick the leaf around the stem stick. Finally, put a little glue onto the base of the second leaf and stick the leaf onto the stem, opposite the first leaf.

Glue

Paintbrush

Poster paint

Petals

9

LAUGHING CLOWN CARD

Make this happy pop-up card for someone special. Start by tracing all the pattern pieces from page 29 using a pencil.

page 29

YOU WILL NEED

Large sheet of brightly colored construction paper

White, red, and orange paper

Three other colors of paper for clothes

Sequin waste (or patterned giftwrapping paper)

Black marking pen

Round paper stickers

Tracing paper

Pencil

All-purpose glue

Scissors

1 From the large sheet of colored paper, measure and cut a rectangle 17in × 11in. Fold it into quarters, folding widthways both times. Your finished card should be 8½in × 5½in.

2 Fold the white paper in half. Turn your pattern tracing face down on top, lining up the straight edge of the head pattern with the fold. Retrace over the head outline so that the shape appears on the paper. Cut it out through both layers.

3 Fold the nose up to the side as shown below to crease it. Open out the head and push the nose through to the front. Recrease the front of the nose.

4 Fold the other colored papers in half and retrace the pattern shapes onto them, lining up the straight edges against the folds as before. Cut out all the pieces through both layers of paper. Use the pattern to cut a bow from sequin waste.

5 Glue the square red mouth piece onto the back of the head. Turn the head over and draw on the eyes with a pen. Glue the mouth and nose into place.

6 Fold the hair back along the dotted line to make a crease. Cut the fringe. Open out the hair and push the fringe to the front as shown below. Stick the hair onto the head.

7 Open the card out flat. Stick the body inside and decorate it with paper stickers. Then glue the collar and the head in place. Finally, glue the bowtie together and stick it in place under the clown's chin.

Hair

Head

Card

Folding nose

Nose

Mouth

Bowtie

Clothes

Pen

Scissors

Mouth piece in place

Glue

FLOWER GARLAND

Make a tropical garland to give to party guests, or to
go with a Hallowe'en costume. This one is made from
16 flowers, but you can make yours longer if you like.

1 For each flower, cut 15 or so circles from crepe paper. To cut out the circles quickly, you can cut through several layers of paper at once. Using a pen, draw around a circular lid onto a strip of folded crepe paper.

2 Hold the paper firmly together and cut out the circle through all the layers. Repeat until you have enough flowers. You will need eight of each color.

3 Holding all the layers of a flower firmly together, cut short snips into the circle with your scissors to make the petals. Cut petals in the other flowers in the same way.

4 Now make some stalks for your garland out of straws. Cut the straws into 2in lengths. You will need 16 pieces in all.

Crepe paper circles

5 Thread the needle with a long piece of thread, and knot the end several times to make a large knot. Push the needle through the center of each paper circle until you have threaded one flower, then thread on a straw. Now thread on another, different colored flower, and another straw. Continue until all the flowers and straws are strung together.

Straws

6 Unthread the needle and tie the two thread ends together into a secure knot. Push the thread ends into a straw to finish.

7 To make the leaves, cut 16 strips of green crepe paper about 1in × 5in. Cut the ends into points. Then tie each strip around a straw, close to a flower, finishing off with a double knot.

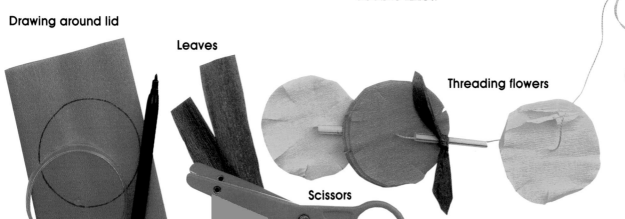

Drawing around lid

Leaves

Threading flowers

Needle and thread

Scissors

13

Mouse Mask

This cute mouse mask is just the thing for a Hallowe'en party. Begin by tracing the pattern from page 30 using a pencil. Complete the head by turning your tracing over and drawing the other half.

1 Turn your tracing face down onto the white cardboard and retrace over the head and nose outlines. Turn the tracing over as before to complete the head. The shapes will appear on the cardboard. Cut them out.

2 Retrace the teeth pattern onto the cream paper and the ear and nose tip onto the pink. Cut them out. Then trace and cut out a second ear.

3 Cut a hole in the middle of the head as marked on the pattern. Draw small circles for the eyes with a compass and punch a hole in the center of each one. Color in the eyes with a black pen.

4 Fold back the tab on the teeth as marked. Glue the tab onto the head. Now cut out three narrow strips of black paper about 10in long. Glue them in place for the whiskers.

5 Stick the nose tip onto the nose. Turn the nose over and, using a ruler and a knitting needle, mark heavily down the fold lines to crease, or score, the paper. Fold the nose into shape and glue it onto the head.

6 Score the fold lines in the ears and fold the corners over. Glue the ears onto the back of the head. Finally, make small holes in the sides of the mask with a darning needle; thread the elastic through and finish off with a knot.

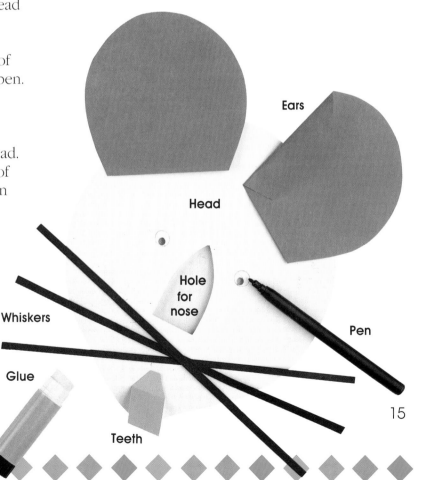

Ears

Head

Hole for nose

Round elastic

Nose

Compass

Whiskers

Glue

Pen

Teeth

15

WOVEN BASKETS

Weave a small paper basket to hold gifts, or use it to keep your desk tidy. Choose bright colors to show the woven strips to the best effect.

YOU WILL NEED

Construction paper in four
　　colors – green, yellow,
　　orange, and red
Ruler
Set square
Pencil
Scissors
All-purpose glue

1 Using a ruler and set square, draw a 6¾in square on red paper and cut it out. Draw a line 1½in in from each side to make a border. Mark the center square into ¾in wide strips. (There is a diagram on page 31 for you to follow.)

2 Cut five strips of 14in × ⅝in paper for weaving – you'll need two green, two yellow and one orange. Then cut a longer green strip, 18in × ⅝in, to bind the basket edge.

Cutting strips in base

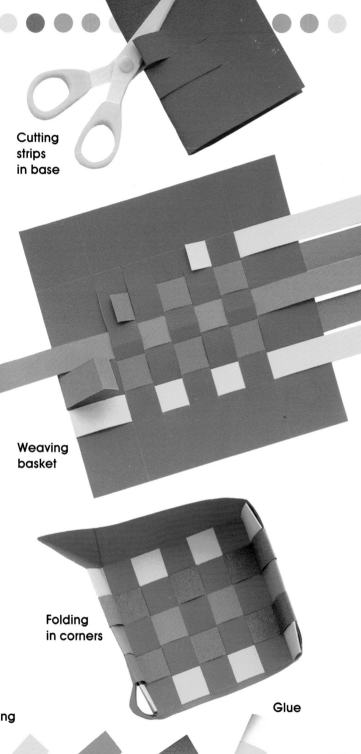

3 Fold the square in half and cut along the drawn lines up to the border lines as shown. Open out flat and weave the strips in and out of the basket base. When you have woven a strip through, fold the ends over and slot them back into the weave on the other side, trimming the ends as necessary.

4 Fold the border up around the woven center square, forming the corners into triangle shapes as shown. Fold the corners into points and tuck them back into the weave.

Weaving basket

5 Cut an orange strip 14in × ⅝in for the handle. Weave one end into the base of the basket. Loop the handle over the basket and weave it back into the base on the other side. Glue the sides of the handle to the basket. Finally, weave the long green strip around the outside edge of the basket and glue the ends together.

Folding in corners

Glue

Strips for weaving

17

BIRD MOBILE

Brighten up your bedroom with this chirpy mobile. First, trace the pattern of shapes from page 31 using a pencil.

YOU WILL NEED

(To make six birds)
Construction paper in three
    bright colors
Small bead
Black marking pen
Tracing paper
Pencil
Paper punch
Compass
Ruler
Scissors
Paper glue
Thick colored thread
Needle

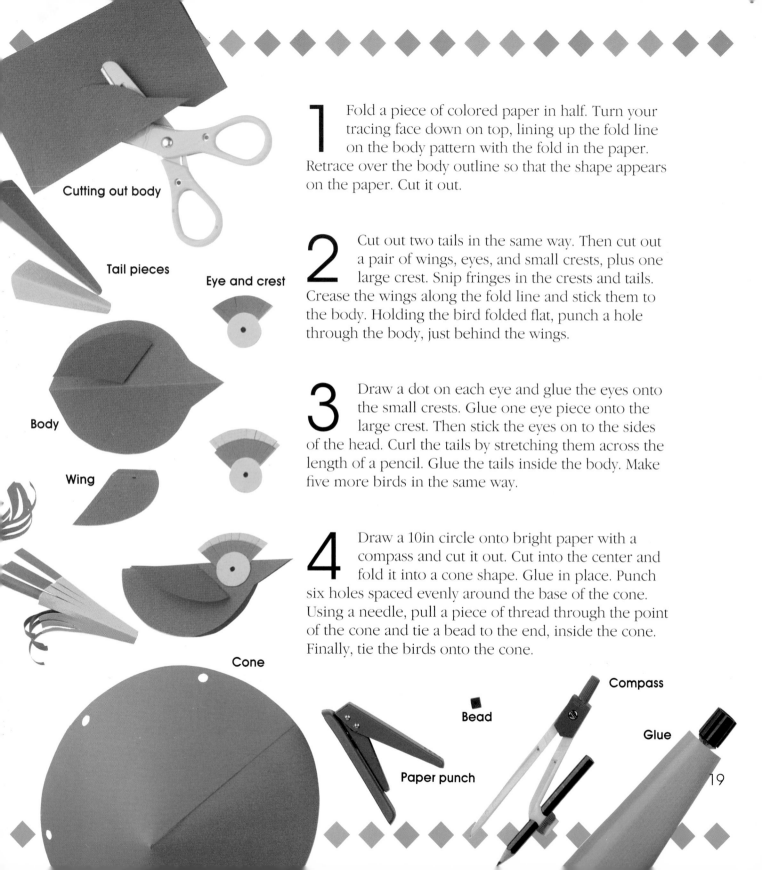

Cutting out body

Tail pieces

Eye and crest

Body

Wing

Cone

1 Fold a piece of colored paper in half. Turn your tracing face down on top, lining up the fold line on the body pattern with the fold in the paper. Retrace over the body outline so that the shape appears on the paper. Cut it out.

2 Cut out two tails in the same way. Then cut out a pair of wings, eyes, and small crests, plus one large crest. Snip fringes in the crests and tails. Crease the wings along the fold line and stick them to the body. Holding the bird folded flat, punch a hole through the body, just behind the wings.

3 Draw a dot on each eye and glue the eyes onto the small crests. Glue one eye piece onto the large crest. Then stick the eyes on to the sides of the head. Curl the tails by stretching them across the length of a pencil. Glue the tails inside the body. Make five more birds in the same way.

4 Draw a 10in circle onto bright paper with a compass and cut it out. Cut into the center and fold it into a cone shape. Glue in place. Punch six holes spaced evenly around the base of the cone. Using a needle, pull a piece of thread through the point of the cone and tie a bead to the end, inside the cone. Finally, tie the birds onto the cone.

Bead

Compass

Glue

Paper punch

Pleated Fans

These pretty paper fans will keep you cool on hot summer days. Decorate them using a paper punch to make a lacy pattern, or use paper doilies and gold giftwrapping paper for an old-fashioned look. We have used square doilies but you can use round ones instead.

Scissors

1 First, cut a strip of paper about 10in × 27in. Use a ruler and set square to help you measure accurately. If your paper is not long enough, stick several shorter pieces together.

2 Use a ruler and pencil to draw lines across your paper ¾in apart. Using a knitting needle, redraw over the lines, pressing down firmly to crease, or score, the paper. Now pleat your fan.

3 Cut two more paper strips, 5in and 3½in wide. Pleat them as before, then punch holes along one long edge of each strip.

4 Lay the wider pleated strip over the fan, lining up the pleats. Stick it in place with a drop of glue behind each pleat, top and bottom. Now stick the smaller strip in place.

5 Measure and cut out two paper strips 10in × ¾in. Stick one strip onto each end of the fan to strengthen and neaten the edges.

Paper punch

6 Gather up the fan and put a drop of glue at the base of each pleat, front and back. Wrap a rubber band around the base to hold it together until the glue is dry. Cut a 2in wide strip of paper long enough to wrap around the handle. Glue it in place. Decorate the handle with a narrower strip in the same way.

7 To decorate your fan with paper doilies, stick the doilies onto the fan before you pleat it. Stick a strip of gold giftwrapping paper across the bottom of the doilies. Then pleat the fan. Add side strips and a handle as described in steps five and six. Finish off by tying giftwrapping ribbon around the handle.

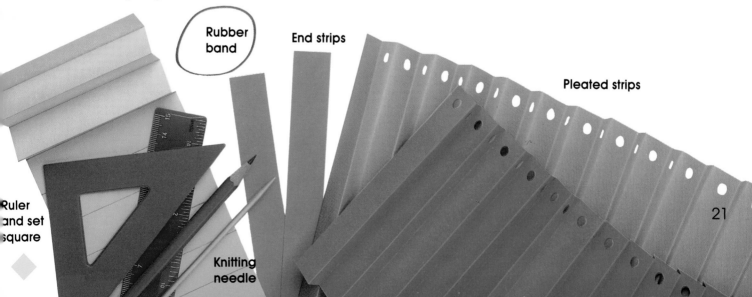

Rubber band

End strips

Pleated strips

Ruler and set square

Knitting needle

21

FUN FINGER PUPPETS

Stage your own show with this cheerful trio of finger puppets. We have made an elephant, a chicken, and a porcupine, but all kinds of animals can be made using the basic cone shape. So use your imagination and make a lot of different performers.

YOU WILL NEED

Brightly colored paper
Tracing paper
Pencil
Paper glue
All-purpose glue
Scissors
Pair of rolley eyes for each
    puppet
Small black bead for
    porcupine's nose

1 For each puppet, trace the body shape from page 32 using a pencil. Turn your tracing face down onto the colored paper and carefully retrace over the outline. The shape will appear on the paper. Cut it out.

2 Wrap the body into a cone shape and stick the overlapping edges together with paper glue. Hold the join together between your finger and thumb until the glue is completely dry.

3 Now trace the other pattern shapes from page 32. Transfer the shapes onto different colored paper as before and cut out all the pieces.

4 Using paper glue, stick the wings onto the sides of the chicken and the tail inside the base. Put a little glue around the point of the body and wrap the beak around it; stick the overlapping edges down.

5 Glue the porcupine's ears in place and make quills out of triangles of colored paper. Glue the ears and trunk onto the elephant's body.

6 Finally, using all-purpose glue, stick rolley eyes onto each puppet and the bead onto the porcupine's nose.

Glue

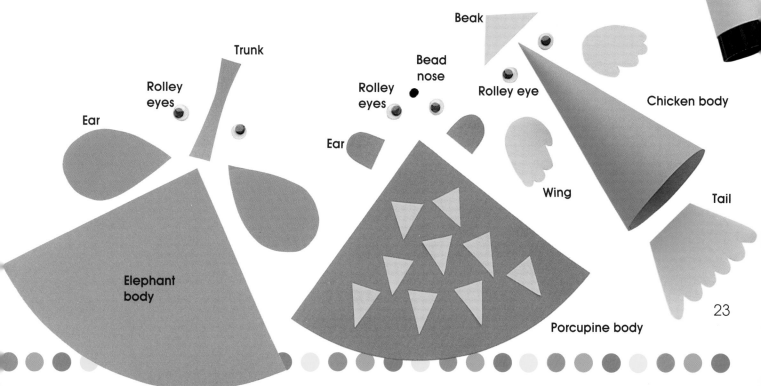

Trunk

Rolley eyes

Ear

Beak

Bead nose

Rolley eyes

Ear

Rolley eye

Chicken body

Wing

Tail

Elephant body

Porcupine body

23

MONKEY BOOKMARK

This useful monkey bookmark will help you find
your place every time. Make him out of colored
construction paper and simply fold his arms over
the corner of your page to mark the spot.
You will find all the pattern pieces on page
32 of this book. Begin by tracing
all the shapes with a pencil.

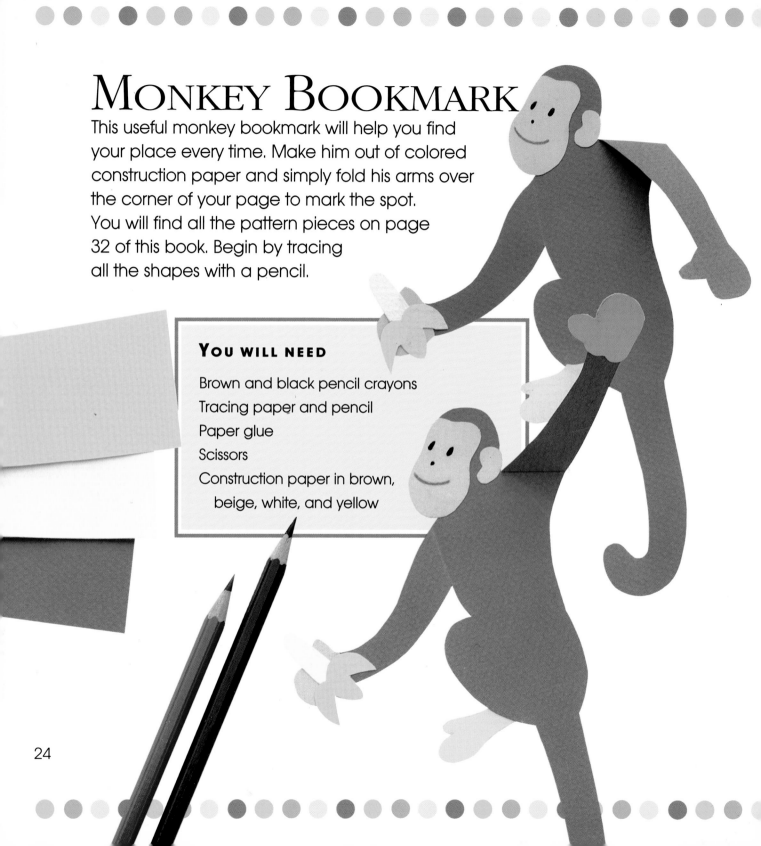

YOU WILL NEED

Brown and black pencil crayons
Tracing paper and pencil
Paper glue
Scissors
Construction paper in brown,
    beige, white, and yellow

1 Turn your tracing face down onto the brown paper and retrace over the monkey's body. Trace the face, ear, feet, and hands onto beige paper – you will need to draw two hands. Trace the banana onto white paper and the peel onto yellow. Now cut out all the shapes.

2 Mark the fold lines across the top of the monkey's arms. Fold the arms over and press the fold down with your thumb to make a crease. Open the arms out flat again.

3 Using paper glue, stick the face, ears and hands in place on the front of the monkey's body. Stick the feet in place on the back of the body.

4 Stick the white of the banana on top of the right hand. Then glue the banana skin over the banana. Look at the picture on the opposite page to make sure you have glued all the pieces in the right place.

5 To finish your bookmark, draw the monkey's eyes and nose onto the face with a black pencil crayon. Use a brown pencil crayon to draw his mouth.

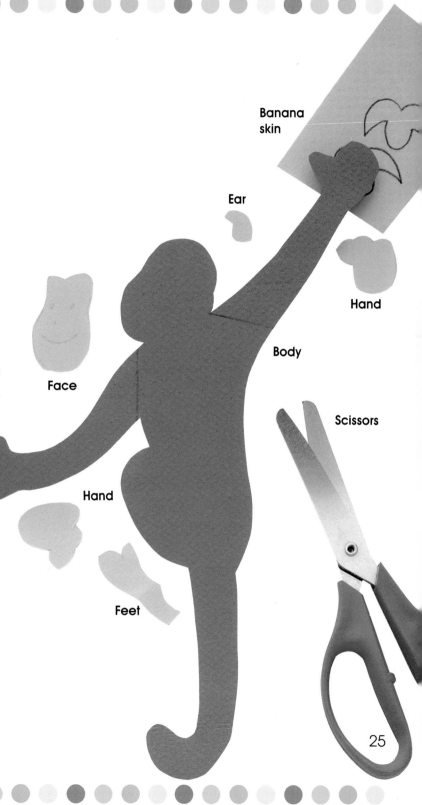

Banana skin

Ear

Hand

Body

Face

Scissors

Hand

Feet

A Handmade Book

Make your own special book to use as a scrapbook or notebook. You can make it any size, with as many pages as you like, in any color you choose. Decorate the cover with giftwrapping paper or cut-outs of a favorite character, or with your own drawings.

You will need

White and colored paper
  for pages
Thin cardboard for cover
Giftwrapping paper
Colored raffia or yarn
Pencil
Ruler
Set square
Paper punch
Knitting needle
Large darning
  needle
Paper glue
Scissors

1 Here's how to make the large book. Start by making the pages. Draw 10in × 8in rectangles on your paper, using a ruler and set square to measure the sizes accurately. Then cut out all the pages. On one long side of every page, make a mark 3in in from each end. Punch a hole at these points.

2 Cut two 10½in × 8¼in covers from cardboard. On both covers, draw a line down one long side, 1in in from the edge. Using a ruler and knitting needle, draw over the lines to crease the cardboard.

3 Cut two pieces of giftwrapping paper a little larger all around than the covers, then glue them onto the scored side of the covers. Press the paper well into the creases. Trim away the extra paper.

4 Cut two strips 1in wide and 11in long from bright paper. Stick these over the creased edges and trim the ends level. Punch holes 3¼in in from each end.

5 Make protective corner covers from the same bright paper. Cut four strips of paper 2in × 4¾in. For each corner, fold the strip in the middle as shown below, then trim the ends. Glue the corners onto the covers.

6 Place the pages between the covers, making sure the punched holes line up. Thread the needle with raffia, then thread the raffia through the two sets of holes in the book. Tie a double knot or a neat bow, and trim the ends.

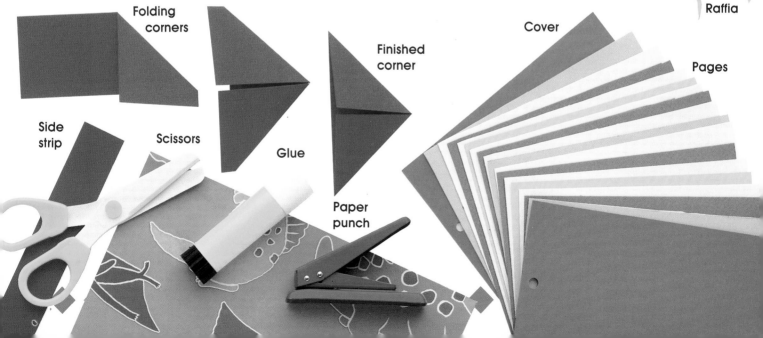

Folding corners

Side strip

Scissors

Glue

Finished corner

Paper punch

Cover

Pages

Raffia

PATTERNS

PAPER FLOWERS
Page 8

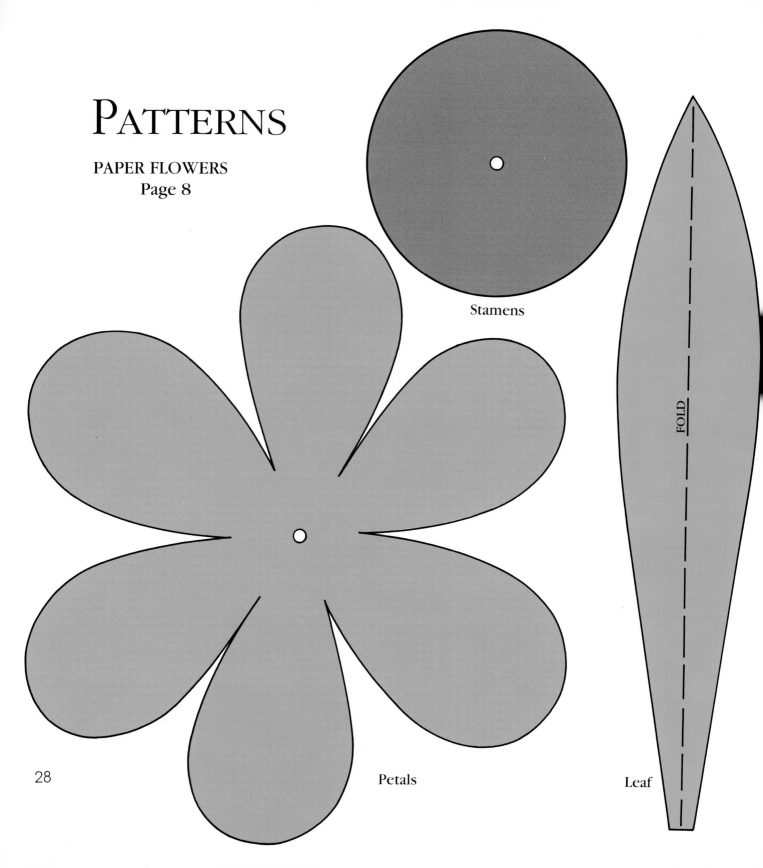

Stamens

FOLD

28

Petals

Leaf

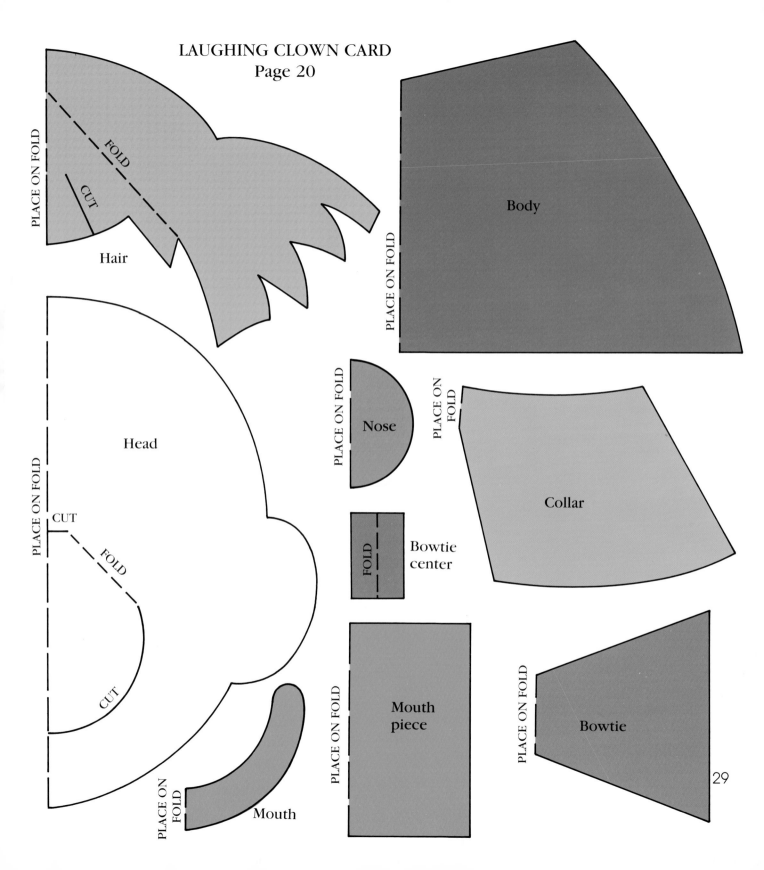

LAUGHING CLOWN CARD
Page 20

Hair

PLACE ON FOLD

FOLD

CUT

Body

PLACE ON FOLD

Head

PLACE ON FOLD

CUT

FOLD

CUT

Nose

PLACE ON FOLD

Collar

PLACE ON FOLD

FOLD

Bowtie center

Mouth piece

PLACE ON FOLD

Bowtie

PLACE ON FOLD

Mouth

PLACE ON FOLD

29

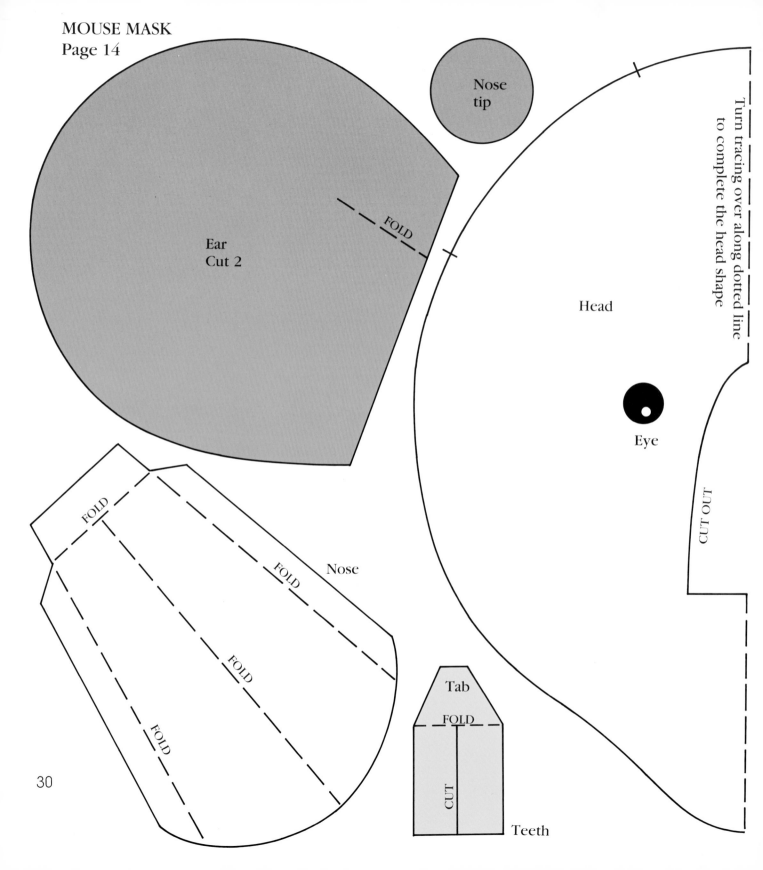

MOUSE MASK
Page 14

Nose
tip

Turn tracing over along dotted line
to complete the head shape

Ear
Cut 2

FOLD

Head

Eye

CUT OUT

FOLD

FOLD

Nose

FOLD

FOLD

Tab

FOLD

CUT

Teeth

30

WOVEN BASKETS Page 16

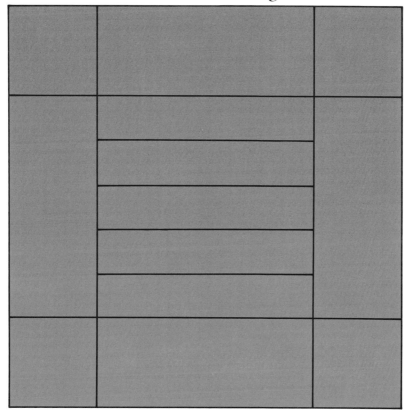

BIRD MOBILE
Page 18

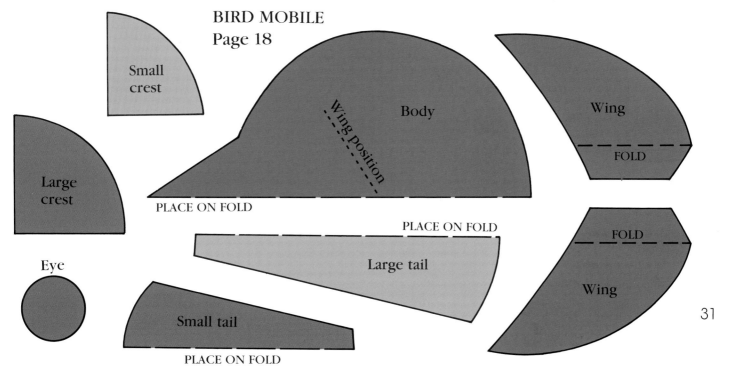

Small crest

Large crest

Eye

Body

Wing position

PLACE ON FOLD

Wing

FOLD

PLACE ON FOLD

Large tail

Small tail

FOLD

Wing

PLACE ON FOLD

31

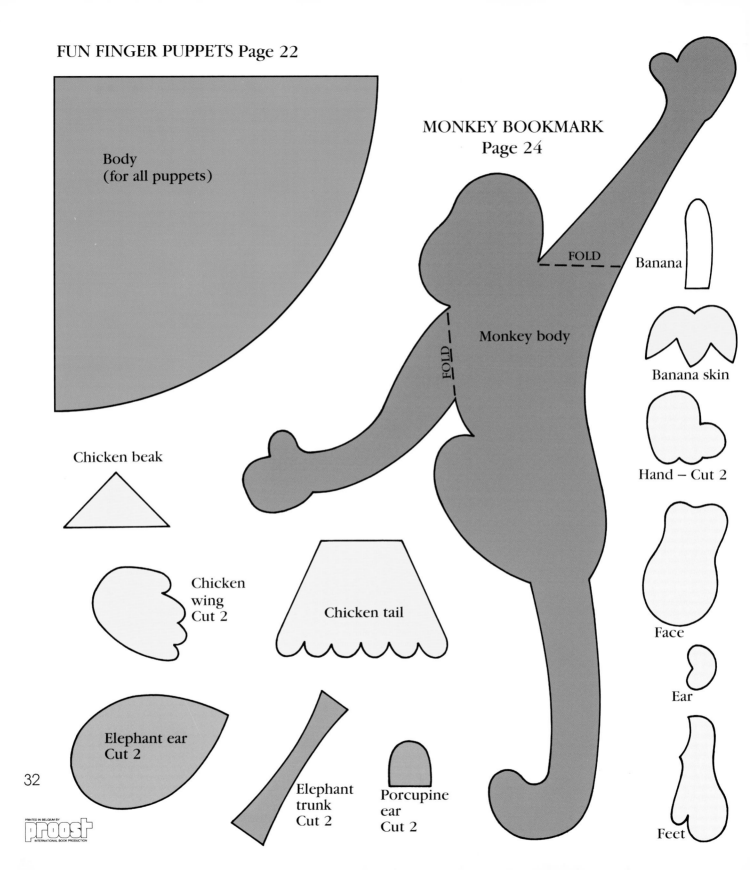

FUN FINGER PUPPETS Page 22

Body
(for all puppets)

MONKEY BOOKMARK
Page 24

FOLD

Banana

Banana skin

Monkey body

FOLD

Hand – Cut 2

Chicken beak

Face

Chicken
wing
Cut 2

Chicken tail

Ear

Elephant ear
Cut 2

Elephant
trunk
Cut 2

Porcupine
ear
Cut 2

Feet

32